If you find this

K.E.S.

And someone will come to retrieve it.

Thank you!

Buddha Meditations

A Journal

Edited by Susan Brassfield Cogan

ISBN-9781520384436

Printed in the United States of America

Published by Coganbooks

Cover and Book Design by:
Cogan Graphic Design
www.cogangraphicdesign.com

Text from:
The Hands of the Buddha
Edited by Susan Brassfield Cogan
available at http://bit.ly/Coganbooks

How to Use this Journal

Of course, you can use this journal any way you like! You can scribble limericks, keep grocery lists, or review old television shows.

But! You can use each page as a "thought for the day" and then ignore the quotes and use the lined pages as a record of your daily journey.

You can doodle on the left page under the quote or you can cut pictures out of magazines and glue them there.

You can use the quotes as writing prompts.

The Buddha once said "Do not believe in anything simply because you have heard it. ... Do not believe in anything simply because it is found written in your religious books. ... But after observation and analysis, when you find that anything agrees with reason and is conducive to the good and benefit of one and all, then accept it and live up to it."

You have permission to argue with the quotes. You can analyze them and see how they fit with your life or not. You can modify them into something more suitable to you.

You can do a mix of all of the above.

This is your book.

We are what we think about. All our lives
are founded on our thoughts and our world
is made up of our thoughts. Like the wagon
drawn after an ox, suffering will follow a
deluded mind.

We are what we think about. When our minds
are clear and disciplined, happiness will follow
us as faithfully as our shadow.

Hatred can not be defeated by hatred. Only love can defeat hatred. This wisdom is as ancient as humanity.

Those who can distinguish between the truth and dreams may live happily in the world as it actually is.

There is no fire like craving. There is no pain like hatred. There is no suffering like attachment or aversion which are two sides of the same coin. There is no joy like liberation, there is no peace like a quiet heart.

Delighting in mindfulness and fearing heedlessness the seeker, with the fire of his attentive mind, burns away bonds both large and small and goes free.

When we learn to enjoy life without grasping after temporary pleasures we can resist the Illusionist, the way a stony mountain resists the wind.

Those who look at a dream and think they see reality and those who look at reality and think they are seeing a dream are afflicted with empty longing.

An untrained mind is like a leaky roof. As rain will drip through a roof full of holes, so will craving pour through an unfocused mind.

Skillful behavior makes all the world an enduring pleasure. When we behave well toward others our lives will be filled with joy.

Behaving well is its own reward and will bring happiness and contentment. The good person can be pleased when they think of the good they do and are happy while they are doing good.

Even if you have read vast amounts of the Dharma, if you don't follow the teachings you are like a person who learns all about cattle but only counts the cows of other people.

Those who understand the importance of mindfulness are happy to pay attention. Those who meditate faithfully and with strong intention will find happiness and well-being.

By devotedly working to awaken and by
training our minds, we can make for ourselves
an island that cannot be flooded.

A wise person who has scaled the heights of awareness, views all those who are still in turmoil with great compassion. From a place of serenity she pays heed to those who still suffer.

Just as a fletcher makes an arrow as straight as possible, so a wise person will work to steady a trembling, flickering mind no matter how difficult and wild it becomes.

Like a fish that has been pulled from the
water and thrown down on the ground
so our minds tremble and fight when
withdrawn from the domination of Mara, the
Illusionist.

A good engineer builds canal to channel water where ever it is needed. Fletchers straighten the arrow, carpenters shape wood into something of use. Followers of the Dharma shape themselves.

If your mind is unsteady, if you don't follow the teachings, your confidence will waiver and wisdom will elude you.

Our bodies are as fragile as a clay jar but if we make our minds as strong as a walled city, we can use wisdom like a sword to keep Mara at bay. Once we have conquered, then a quiet, unattached vigil will keep the city safe.

As much as they love you, your mother, your father and your family cannot give you the blessings you can give yourself with a well-trained mind.

Someone who follows the path of the disciplined mind can see into the true heart of the cosmos. They can discern the teachings as easily as someone can choose a perfect bloom for a garland.

Those who know this body is like bubbles in sea foam and understand that life is a fragile illusion will perceive the flower arrows of Mara and go to the land of life where Mara cannot go.

Some people grasp after transient pleasures like someone picking flowers. While the mind wanders distracted by this color and that blossom, death comes like a flood that carries away a sleeping village.

Without harming the color or fragrance of
the flower, a bee drinks of its nectar. That is
how a wise person dwells in the world.

Don't dwell on what other people do and do not do. Instead try to see what you do and do not do with unjudgmental clarity.

A person who speaks well and beautifully and who performs outward postures but doesn't really follow the wise path is like a showy flower that has no scent.

The scent of lavender, jasmine and sandalwood incense blows this way and that in the breeze, but the fragrance of right action radiates out in all directions.

The scent of sandalwood, jasmine or lotus is faint compared to the perfume of those who practice good deeds and diligently follow the teachings. The fragrance of right actions rises to the heavens.

Just as a beautiful lily full of sweetness and delight can grow in garbage beside the road, a true disciple of the Dharma becomes like a light for people struggling in darkness.

The night is long when you can't sleep. The road is long to the tired traveler. Life is long to those who are mesmerized by illusion.

When traveling the true path, find wise companions or continue on alone. There is no benefit in traveling with a fool.

"These children are mine and this wealth belongs to me." Those are thoughts that torment a fool. If we can't master ourselves, how can we own money or other people?

The fool who understands she is foolish is a little bit wise. But a fool who thinks she is wise, is completely a fool.

Even if a fool studies with a wise teacher for many years, he will still be a fool. He will understand the truth as well as a spoon can taste the soup.

A discerning person can learn volumes after
only spending a moment with a wise teacher.
He will grasp the truth of things the way the
tongue perceives the taste of the soup.

Fools are their own worst enemy. Their willful ignorance bears its own bitter fruit.

A bad deed is something that we later regret. The harvest of such a deed is reaped with tears. A good deed is one which you never regret. We reap the harvest of good deeds with joy and gladness.

Until a bad deed begins to bear fruit the fool thinks it is sweet like honey but when it ripens, the fool knows the bitter fruit of suffering.

It doesn't matter if a fool fasts and lives like an ascetic for months. He doesn't compare in value with someone who has seen into the truth of reality. Asceticism isn't the way.

As fresh milk doesn't curdle immediately, so an evil deed does not go bad right away. It smolders like hot coals in the ashes and waits to burn the fool.

The fool wishes for a grand reputation, to be worshiped and admired. "Let everyone think I did these wonderful things and that I am worthy of praise and rewards." This is the thought of a fool who grasps after self aggrandizement.

One road leads to worldly gain, the other road leads to liberation. One who follows the Buddha will not grasp after gifts and adoration but will seek tranquility and follow the path to freedom.

Avoid confused and immoral people. Instead
look for friends and companions who are
kindhearted, thoughtful and uplifting.

One who drinks deeply of the Dharma will abide in well-being. The wise always rejoice in the wisdom taught by the Buddha.

Just as engineers direct the watercourse
however they want, just as fletchers fashion
the arrow and carpenters work the wood, so
do wise people shape themselves.

Just as a mountain does not tremble and shake in the wind, so are wise people not affected by praise or blame.

The wise do not prattle about shallow pleasures or chase after them. Whether touched by joy or grief, though profoundly intimate with the moment, the wise person is not owned by their emotions.

Few people cross the wide river to find freedom. Most people run up and down the bank afraid to risk the journey. But those who have taken the Dharma to heart and learned it well will cross the stormy sea of passions and reach enlightenment even though the journey is difficult.

A wise person will step out of the dark prison of delusion and seek the path of light even though there are no walls or roof. Wandering without clinging to the illusion of security and stability is difficult but it is the only way to freedom.

Those whose minds are well grounded in
the Dharma, who live without clinging will
rejoice in freedom from attachment. When
they have seen through all the illusions and
released all grasping they will wake up.

Having journeyed to the end of the Dharma Path at last, the Awakened Ones abide without the shackles of illusion, free of suffering and grief. The Awakened travel without a thought of home. They escape the illusion of permanent home like swans arising from the lake

Those who accumulate no goods, who are free of temptations, who have seen into the true nature of the cosmos are truly awake. They walk on the wind like the journey of birds in the sky.

To become awake is to leave behind
confusion. The Awakened abide like the
earth, they stand like a pillar to the sky, they
are a clear pond that reveals quiet depths.
Such a person has creased all suffering.

The Awakened One is free of blind faith but instead sees into the nature of reality. One who has loosened all bonds, is free of all snares and sees neither good nor bad but just one thing is awake.

The splendid carriages of monarchs eventually crumble to dust, just as our bodies do. The Dharma is eternal and continues without failing as long as people of good will are willing to teach people with good hearts.

When the moon emerges from behind the clouds it shines on a darkened world. So it is when someone who was formerly ignorant becomes dis-illusioned.

Making burnt offerings to the gods for a hundred years is useless compared to honoring, for a single moment, a person who has seen into the nature of things.

If you are respectful of elders and those who have gone before, then you will gain four things: health and long life, strength and joy.

A person with an undisciplined and
wandering mind who lives a hundred years
will not be as happy as a person who spends
a single day in mindfulness.

Life is as fragile and temporary as a bubble.
Life is a mirage shimmering in the distance.
If you remember that, you will see through
illusion and Mara will not be able to find
you.

Never set aside your practice to do the work of another even if they tell you their work is very important. Help others, but view your own work as primary. When you have found your Dharma Path, follow it single-mindedly.

If you do something wrong don't dwell on it, but don't repeat that mistake. Only harm comes out of doing harm.

If you do something right, enjoy your
memories of it and make it a habit.
Happiness is the outcome of right action.

Sow ignorance and reap suffering. Sow goodness and reap strength. You are the source of all your strength and weakness. No person can save another.

Don't minimize small good deeds. Like a pot eventually filled by raindrops, doing good deeds will become a habit and little by little happiness will saturate your life.

As a merchant who is entrusted with a precious treasure will avoid a dangerous highway, so you should avoid evil. As you love life, avoid poison.

Love yourself and be mindful at all times—
in the misty morning of childhood, in the
hot afternoon of youth, in the cool evening
of old age.

There is no place on earth to hide from evil deeds, no place to hide from death. In the sky, on the ocean, deep in a cave under the mountains—there death and suffering will find you. Knowing this, the wise person always strives to do good in the world.

Everyone is afraid of being harmed and everyone loves life. Remember that everyone is like you and do not harm anyone or cause anyone to die, nor persuade others to do bad deeds.

If someone speaks rudely to you and you are as silent as a broken gong, then you have reached freedom and you'll never respond in kind.

I have looked long in vain for whoever built this house. Now I have found you O Builder and I have broken down the walls, smashed in the door and I have dug up the foundations. I have found the end of craving.

Shakyamuni has flown like a heron from the snare. His conquest is greater than the earth. Gautama has conquered himself. He has become still. Buddha is Awake.

Made in the USA
Middletown, DE
09 October 2017